D1520410

Roger Williams

REAL PEOPLE

ROGER WILLIAMS

By JOSEPH COTTLER

Illustrated by JACOB LANDAU

FRANCES CAVANAH, *Director of Biographies*

-7117

JB
W

3-27-56

ROW, PETERSON AND COMPANY
EVANSTON, ILLINOIS   WHITE PLAINS, NEW YORK

The Boy Who Thought for Himself

Roger thought that no church in London gave out lovelier chimes than his own church, Saint Sepulchre's (sep'ul-kerz). There was a song about the bells of London which went:

> " 'Kettles and pans,'
> Say the bells at St. Ann's.
> 'You owe me five farthings,'
> Say the bells at St. Martin's.
> 'When will you pay me?'
> Say the bells at Old Bailey.
> 'When I grow rich,'
> Say the bells at Shoreditch.
> 'Pray when will that be?'
> Say the bells at Stepney.
> 'I'm sure I don't know,'
> Says the great bell at Bow."

Silly song! The solemn dong-a-dong did not say, "When will you pay me"—not to the boy Roger Williams. The sound carried him far away from the clink of money and the life around him. "Somewhere," the bells seemed to say, "there is a world happier than this one. In that world there are no tears because nobody ever hurts another person. Go seek that happy world, Roger."

Whenever Roger first stepped inside the church, the sudden hush of light hid the altar. But he knew that it was there, and when his eyes became used to the dim light, he could see the altar at the end of the deep nave. Seated beside his father and mother, he waited for the service to begin. While they turned the pages of their Bibles, he drew out a paper

and pencil. He had learned to take down the sermon in that rapid kind of writing known as shorthand. In the sermon Roger usually felt echoes of the song of the bells. He seemed to hear the message of a happier world.

One Sunday, when the preacher had finished, Roger was about to roll up his page. "How now, boy," a voice above him said, "what unholy magic is this that you practice in church?"

An elderly man was looking over his shoulder. Roger's father rose, and his mother made a little curtsy. "Good morrow, Sir Edward," said Mr. Williams. "May I have the honor to present my son Roger? He knows how to write in shorthand."

Mr. Williams snatched the paper out of Roger's hand and gave it to Sir Edward. The old gentleman looked hard at the page of hooks and dashes which Roger had made.

"Bless me," murmured Sir Edward. Then he thrust the paper at the boy, pointing to one line with a crooked finger. "What does it say there, right there, in Christian words?" he asked.

Roger promptly read the line. "And may the eyes of His Majesty be opened that he may behold the corruption in the land."

"Bless me," said Sir Edward again. He put his hand on Roger's shoulder. "You could be very useful to me at court and earn a penny or two besides."

That meeting was the beginning of Roger's friendship with Sir Edward Coke. It was a lucky day for Roger. Soon afterwards he went to work for Sir Edward, who was the greatest judge in the kingdom and a leader in Parliament. Parliament was the group of men who made some of the laws for Great Britain. They still had very little power, but more and more they were demanding the right to help the king rule the country and its colonies.

Roger Williams had been born in the city of London about 1603. His father was a merchant and tailor whose shop took up the front downstairs room of the Williams home. This home was a two-storied gabled house in Cow Lane, a fine new street near the northern limits of London town. Roger lived about half a mile from the Thames (*temz*) River, and a brisk three-minute walk brought him to the open country.

Here almost every day of the week some market was going on. Tuesday it was a horse fair. The next day pigs or cattle might be sold there, or perhaps it was a hay market. Some-

times a row of booths was set up, and the cloth merchants of the city displayed their wares. At such times Roger went with his father. Mr. Williams passed along the booths, stopping at each one and rubbing the cloth between his fingers.

There was one season of the year when the grounds were given over to sports, such as wrestling. Best of all Roger liked the shows. There was one show in which he saw a cavern with a fire burning inside. Above it the sign read: "Mouth of Hell." Out of the cavern, to everyone's delight, would spring a clown dressed as the devil. Behind him little demons, with hair pasted all over their clothes, ran around the field crying, "Ho! Ho!"

These country grounds were not always the scene of business or sport. Once, on that very spot, a tragedy had taken place. In 1612, when Roger was about nine years old, a preacher had been burned to death. Not by accident. James I, the king of England, had ordered that the man should be burned at the stake.

"But why?" Roger had asked.

His father's face was grim as he replied: "The man was a heretic. The archbishop said so."

"What is a heretic, Father?" Roger insisted.

"One who doesn't believe as the king and his bishops believe," was the reply.

"Do we believe as the king or his bishops?"

Mr. Williams hesitated. "We are all Christians, Roger," he finally said.

"Well, I don't believe as the king does," declared Roger.

"Quiet, boy."

All the same Roger knew that he was living in troubled times. He saw the frowns when his father talked with friends about James I and the elegant courtiers who lived at his court. They spent huge sums of money for their silks and furs and beautiful jewels, and they wore their hair long under their fine feathered hats.

They looked very different from some of the people Roger saw at St. Sepulchre's. At St. Sepulchre's many of the members wore dark simple clothes and cut their hair short. They worked hard during the week and considered Sunday a time for prayer. The elegant courtiers scoffed at such serious people, calling them "Puritans." The boy Roger became a Puritan. More and more Londoners joined the Puritans in opposing the king. The majority of the members of Parliament, whose leader was Sir Edward Coke, were on the side of the Puritans.

"I shall drive these people out of my land," the king cried, his voice shaking with anger.

He meant what he said. Many people had to flee England and find refuge in a foreign land. Some took refuge in Holland. Others who dared speak out against the king or his bishops were put to death. Some were thrown into prison.

Even so famous a person as Sir Edward Coke had been in prison for a time. He was released only because the king could not always afford to be high and mighty toward a leader in Parliament. For like any other extravagant person, King James usually needed money. From time to time he had to call Parliament together and ask for a loan. At such times the leaders of Parliament would insist on more rights for the plain people of England.

"Sire," they said, "this people will not grant this money unless in return you grant them more liberty."

The king treated Parliament with scorn and suspicion. Parliament watched the king with suspicion and anger.

After young Roger Williams went to work for Sir Edward Coke, he learned a great deal about the trouble stirring in England. Day after day he took down in shorthand the speeches which were made in Sir Edward's law court.

To reach the law court Roger used to walk along the river. Sometimes he passed a barge from which was being unloaded a shipment of weed from Virginia. Virginia was the name of a part of the New World which England claimed. The weed was called "tobacco." The red men of America, it seemed, burned it in a bowl to which a stem was attached. They put the hollow stem between their lips and—strange to tell—drew the smoke of the burning weed into their mouths. Then they would blow it out again immediately. This savage custom was spreading through Europe, and English merchants were growing rich selling tobacco.

The king had issued a charter to a company of merchants, giving them permission to send a colony of Englishmen over to Virginia. A member of St. Sepulchre's, Captain John Smith, had been in charge of the colony for a time. It was the Virginia colony that produced tobacco for sale in Europe. Captain Smith's young Indian friend, Pocahontas, had visited London the year that Roger was thirteen. As he stood in a crowd waiting for her coach to pass by, little did he dream that one day he would have many Indian friends in America. It did not enter his mind that one day he would choose exile in the wilderness to living in England.

Four years later Roger heard that the English refugees in Holland—the people who were later called Pilgrims—had sailed for the New World. That same year, 1620, Roger's father died. Roger was seventeen and quite ready to carry on his father's business, but Sir Edward had a different plan for him.

"My son," said Sir Edward, and Roger thrilled at the word, "my son, you are a born scholar, not a merchant. Would you not care to continue your education?"

Roger hesitated just long enough to talk with his mother. When he learned that she was well provided for, he gratefully said "Yes" to Sir Edward.

"Very well," said Sir Edward. "I am one of the directors of the school at Charterhouse. There is a place waiting for you."

At Charterhouse, Roger's day began at five in the morning. He arose and put on his uniform. The uniform included knee breeches, a short black jacket, an Eton collar, and over all, a gown with wide sleeves. First, he went to chapel exercises. Then after cleaning his room, he reviewed his lessons. At eight o'clock he breakfasted on bread, cheese, and beer. Supper was the same. Dinner was usually a meat and bread pudding. The rest of the day was given to study. Roger made such an excellent record that after three years he was given a scholarship to Cambridge University. Among the students was another young man who one day was to become famous as a poet. His name was John Milton.

Before students graduated from the university, they were asked to take an oath. They must promise to follow the king in their belief and their religion. Most of the boys merely

mumbled the words, hardly realizing what they were saying. When Roger Williams had carefully examined the oath, he was deeply troubled.

"I do not give any man the right to think for me," he thought. "No, not even the king or the archbishop. My religion, all my beliefs, are my own. My beliefs are my conscience."

When Roger was about twenty-six years old, he became a minister. But he felt that preachers could only point the way ahead. To him religion meant a search for a better way of life under God. It was everyone's search. No person could do it for another.

Yet he knew that the king and the archbishop did not approve of persons thinking for themselves about religion. "Believe what we tell you," they ordered. Anyone who refused had to leave England or stay at the risk of his life.

One day a friend of Sir Edward came to Roger and told him that a large company of Puritans was getting ready to sail to America. The king had given them a charter, a permission in writing, to settle in the country of the Massachusetts Indians. This part of America was called New England and lay far north of Virginia. The settlement was to be called Massachusetts Bay Colony. Would Mr. Williams care to join the colony as religious teacher?

Roger Williams hesitated. Leave his native England? Forsake the great city of London for the wilderness? What would Mary Barnard say? Mary was the girl Roger loved. He shook his head.

Then one day the king's officers pounced on a preacher at St. Sepulchre's and put him on trial for speaking his mind. Roger Williams began to think that perhaps only in the wilderness could a man find freedom. Finally he spoke to Mary. He asked if she would go with him.

"I would go with you even to the farthest wilderness," she said simply.

They were married in December of 1629. Still Roger Williams hesitated about taking her to the New World, and the fleet of ships sailed without them. Then suddenly a new political storm swept over England. Charles I, who had become king after his father died, dismissed Parliament. He threw some of its leaders into prison. Roger Williams had no more doubts. He knew that anyone who did not agree with the king might be severely punished—perhaps even put to death.

"If we stay," Roger said to Mary, "I shall not be silent. I intend to preach as my conscience bids me preach."

"Then we had better sail for the New World," said Mary. "I have no wish to be a widow."

Not for an instant did they imagine that the tyranny of the king and his bishops had already spread to the wilderness of America.

Trouble in the New World

The Indians called the place Shawmut, but the white settlers who had taken possession of it called it Boston. To the north, two days' journey through the forest brought the traveler to the cluster of cabins called Salem. To the south lay Plymouth, which had been settled in 1620 by the Pilgrims. In these three little settlements were the people who had lived through the struggle to start new homes in the wilderness. The vast ocean lay on one side, the mysterious forest on the other. But in October of 1635, the settlers' greatest danger lay in their very midst.

Long before dawn on Thursday, October 8, shadows were moving on the trails around Boston. When the sun came up, the shadows turned into hats and long capes, and the whisper of the trees was mixed with English words. Everybody was on his way to Newton Church to attend a meeting of the Massachusetts general court. This day had been set for the trial of Roger Williams, teacher and minister at Salem.

More than five years had passed since Roger and his wife Mary had arrived in New England. He had served as teacher, or pastor, of the church in Salem and had lived for two years in Plymouth. Since he was paid no money for his preaching,

12

he earned his living by trading with the Indians. He had made long trips through their country to buy furs. They trusted him and called him *netop*, the Indian word for friend.

Most of the white settlers also trusted him, but some of the leaders said that he was a dangerous heretic. There was an excited buzz of talk as the people hurried along the trails toward the square wooden church.

The way to the church led past the pillory and the whipping post. The court had condemned many people to be whipped in public or to be branded with hot irons. Sometimes the court condemned a person to be locked in the pillory with his head and hands sticking out. There were cases when the court ordered an ear cut off, but Roger Williams's ears were safe. His crime was considered too great to be paid for by such a simple punishment.

The gloomy church overflowed with people. At one end sat the governor of the colony. Back of him were rows of benches, each row rising higher than the benches in front of it. On these benches sat about fifty grim-looking men. They were magistrates or judges. They made the laws for the colony. Among them were men who thought that it was a sin to take a walk on Sunday. They made it a crime for "humble" people to wear certain clothes or to eat certain foods which the judges said were suitable only for "better" people. But the "crime" of which Roger Williams was accused was considered much more serious.

Roger Williams stood facing his judges, his brown eyes intent upon them, his jaw firmly set. The governor arose. He began by saying that Mr. Williams was a brilliant preacher who had gone astray. For years the court had warned him to mend his ways. He had refused, and the court could no longer put up with his rebellion. The governor accused Mr. Williams on the following counts:

Mr. Williams preached that the government had no authority over the religious opinions of its people. He claimed, for instance, that no magistrate had the right to punish a man for breaking the Sabbath. He even claimed that every man had the right to worship as he wished. Mr. Williams also preached that the English had no right to take the land of the Indians without paying them for it.

The governor asked whether Mr. Williams would take back his words and beg forgiveness. If not, was he ready to defend himself?

"I am ready," said Roger Williams.

Of course, he was ready. That young man had not been permitted to sit in the court of the great judge, Sir Edward Coke,

for nothing. Roger had learned some things there. Yet he
knew that his case was hopeless. The fifty men opposite him
were both the church and the civil government. These men
who accused him were also the judges who would decide
whether he was innocent or guilty. What chance had he? Yet
he had left England for the sake of freedom.

"Here in the New World," he thought bitterly, "I had
hoped to find the right to my own conscience. And this is the
result."

The governor sat down, and a spokesman for the court arose.
The trial began.

The day wore on, and the sun went down while the debate
on freedom was held. Many words were spoken, but the case
was really very simple. Roger Williams had preached that every
man had a right to his own faith so long as he did nobody any
harm. The frowns on the faces of the judges grew deeper.

The governor arose to pronounce sentence. "Mr. Williams," he read, "shall depart out of this jurisdiction within six weeks."

Those words meant that Roger Williams was banished! He must leave Massachusetts Bay Colony.

The news traveled like a shock through the settlements. At Salem the members of Roger Williams's church were indignant. They asked him to continue his preaching. Every Sunday they flocked to hear him. The weeks glided by.

As the hour of exile approached, Mr. Williams's household became the scene of several dramas. First, a baby girl was born. She was Roger and Mary's second child. The little two-year-old daughter, Mary, looked on curiously as her parents bent over the tiny form.

"What shall we name the little pet?" asked the mother. "Roger, how do you like Priscilla?"

The father shook his head.

"Hester?"

The father still shook his head.

"Hepzibah?"

"No."

The mother gave up in despair. "You're hard to suit," she said. "The little thing must have some name."

"She shall have a wonderful name," said the father, lifting the small bundle, "the most wonderful name in life. She shall be called Freeborn—Freeborn Williams."

The parents' joy was darkened by the knowledge that Roger Williams soon would have to leave his wife and little ones. He must find a home somewhere in the forest until they could join him.

Winter struck early that year, with great blasts of wind and heavy snows. One morning Roger Williams woke, feeling ill. During the day his fever mounted, and he took to his bed. This was an awkward time to be sick, but he felt sure that the court would give him time to recover.

Late one evening there was a knock at the door. A neighbor rushed in breathlessly with sudden and secret news. The court, it seemed, had changed its verdict. The magistrates were alarmed because Mr. Williams was so popular. They feared

that if he were permitted to remain anywhere in America, he would attract followers. He would still be a danger to the Massachusetts colony. There was a ship waiting offshore. The court had therefore decided to arrest Mr. Williams and send him back to England at once. There the king would deal with him.

Sick or not, Roger Williams could not delay any longer. He hurriedly arranged with friends to look after his little family. He kissed Mary and the babies good-by. Then he plunged into the forest just as the snow began to fall again.

Democracy Comes to the New World

Along the narrow forest path Roger Williams pushed his way. The snow did not blind him as much as his tears for the cruelty of men. He was bewildered and alone in a frozen forest. Guided by his pocket compass, he walked south and west. His only hope was to reach the Indian village of Massasoit (*mas'ah-soit'*). Massasoit was a friendly sachem (*say'chem*), or chief, whom he had met while trading with the Indians.

The days were hard, but the nights were frightening. Then Roger's chilled limbs would gladly have sunk down in the snow. He knew that if he fell into a sleep he might never rise again. He resisted the desire to rest and stumbled on. He felt that he was being guided by the compass of his spirit toward that happier world where no man hurts another.

Then one day, more dead than alive, he was startled by a call. "What cheer, *netop!*" A group of Massasoit's braves were looking down at him from the top of a large rock. He sank down, not able to take another step. Soon he felt friendly arms around him. He was carried to Massasoit's wigwam, where a roaring fire, rest, and plenty of food restored him.

Massasoit was delighted that the white sachem who could speak the Indians language was going to stay. But the white sachem had come at a bitter time. The sachems, Canonicus (*kah-nahn'ih-kus*) and Massasoit, had fallen out. Scalping knives were being sharpened for a bloody war. Canonicus was chief of a tribe who lived a little farther west around Narragansett (*nair'ah-gan'set*) Bay.

"No, no," cried the white sachem. "Why do you want to make war? What are all the wars of this world about but for greater dishes and bowls of porridge?"

Massasoit replied that he did
not want to fight. It was Canon-
icus who had started the trouble. Roger Williams rose at
once and set out for the camp of Canonicus, who was also a
netop of his.

"Well," said Canonicus, "it isn't I that want to fight.
Massasoit started it."

Roger Williams talked and argued. At last his common sense
and the love which both of the chiefs felt for him brought
results. They smoked the pipe of peace together.

For more than three months Roger Williams lived with
Massasoit. The sachem's house was a tent made of poles set in
a circle. The poles were bent together and covered with bark.
The Indian family and Roger Williams slept around the fire,
each on a mat of bark covered with bearskin. Every day the
men went hunting in the forest. Usually they brought back
bear or beaver, which the women cooked and served with
potatoes and hominy.

The air grew mild, and it was spring again. The white sachem was about to explore the land to find a site on which to build a house for his family. He was surprised one day by a visit of four young men from Massachusetts. They, too, had fled the colony. They asked Mr. Williams whether they might cast in their lot with his.

"Come," said Roger Williams, "we poor and persecuted will find a shelter somewhere."

Canonicus felt so grateful to the white sachem that he invited him and his friends to settle in the Narragansett country. The five white men headed west.

It was not easy to find just the right place to start their settlement, and summer and fall went by. But the more Roger Williams saw of the land, the more he rejoiced.

"The Most High," he declared, "has provided this country as a shelter for the poor and persecuted."

One day he found himself at the mouth of the Moshassuck River, which flowed into the Salt River, a part of Narragansett Bay. Heading his canoe up the Moshassuck, he came upon a spring of sweet water. There he landed.

Providence seemed at last to smile on him. The land rose from the riverbank. The explorer followed the rise until he reached the summit of the hill. On the other side the slope fell gently to the edge of the broad Salt River. Round about were woods of oak and cedar, which would be excellent for building houses. The woods were filled with pigeons, turkeys, deer. The two rivers were stocked with fish. There was a good harbor close by where ships could anchor. Yes, Providence was smiling.

"And Providence shall be the name for my future shelter for the poor and persecuted," Roger Williams thought.

He wrote out a legal deed of sale for the land. Since Canonicus could not write, he drew a bow instead of signing his name. His son drew an arrow. Then the white men began to build their houses.

During the summer of 1636, Mary and the two children arrived. Several neighbors from Salem came along, and all together there were a dozen families to begin the new settlement of Providence. During the next two years, others joined them. It was time, thought Roger, to organize a government.

First, he wrote a new deed to the land which Canonicus had given him. He might have divided it and rented or sold the lots. Instead, the deed said that the settlers should share alike in owning it. They agreed to admit new people if the majority of the old settlers voted "Yes."

They also agreed that every settler was to enjoy "freedom of conscience," which meant freedom of speech as well as freedom of religion. Every person in Providence was to be free to say what he wished and to worship God in the way that he thought right.

Democracy had come to the New World. For the first time anywhere in the world, a government stated simply and clearly

that a person had a right to his beliefs, that no government could tell him how to think. Disputes about property were another matter. These had to be settled according to law. Roger agreed with his neighbors that a committee of five people was to be elected. This committee would hear all disputes and decide what should be done.

Meanwhile, in Boston, the magistrates kept looking for more heretics like Roger Williams. They found Anne Hutchinson, who also preached that each person must follow his own conscience in matters of religion. When she was banished, she and her friends went to Providence. Roger Williams welcomed them and helped them to buy land from Canonicus on a neighboring island.

When more refugees arrived, they also settled near by, and soon the towns of Portsmouth, Newport, and Warwick were founded. All of them followed Providence in setting up a democratic form of government.

For the first few years after Roger Williams left Massachusetts, the magistrates of Boston paid little attention to Providence. They thought that the town would not last, but

instead they saw it grow and flourish. During the year 1638 about twenty ships arrived from England, delivering about three thousand people in New England. The new colonists did not have to settle in Massachusetts. They had the choice of going to Roger Williams's colony. Many of them did go there. Only then did the magistrates of Massachusetts become alarmed. They cried that Providence was a colony of heretics. It was a disease that would spread unless it was stamped out. They decided to appeal to the English king.

The citizens of Providence and the neighboring settlements knew of the hostile feeling toward them. In self-defense they decided to unite and form one colony. In June, 1643, Roger Williams was on the high seas again. He was on his way to London to ask the king for a charter.

As he stood on deck looking out over the gray waters, he thought of all that had happened since he came to America. He had then no idea of founding a colony. When he fled from Massachusetts, through the wilderness, he had hoped to find a home for his family among the Indians. Then other fugitives had joined him, and he had planned a community which offered shelter to all poor and persecuted people. Here every person had the right to live and be free. Only one thing was demanded of a citizen: not to hurt another.

Providence had prospered. But it had powerful enemies. What would happen to the little settlement?

A Refuge for the Poor and Persecuted

By the time Roger Williams arrived in England, the country was in the grip of a civil war. The struggle between king and Parliament had finally become deadly warfare. King Charles I had been driven from London, but his armies still controlled most of England. Parliament was fighting for life. At such a time a dispute between two distant colonies about a charter did not seem very important to English leaders.

Yet Roger Williams presented his case before a commission of Parliament. An agent from Massachusetts was there also to present his side of the case. Then they had to wait for a decision. Roger Williams knew from bitter experience that if the Bay Colony won, he and hundreds like him would again become fugitives in the wilderness.

While waiting he visited his old haunts. The Williams house in Cow Lane had been sold. His mother was dead. Sir Edward Coke had died also. The bells of St. Sepulchre's still clanged stirringly, but the familiar faces were gone from the benches inside.

Roger Williams might have been lonely, but he had work to do. He was writing a book about the American Indians, their language, their way of life. In the book he put his old friends, Massasoit and Canonicus. He told of their kindness

to the English settlers and of the settlers' treachery to them. He wrote:

> "Boast not, proud English, of thy birth and blood,
> Thy brother Indian is by birth as good."

He also wrote: "God has of one blood made all mankind."

The people of England, just then fighting for their liberties, liked Mr. Williams's book. They liked his friendship for the Indians. The men of the Bay Colony, they remembered, had done nothing for the poor Indians. The result was that in March, 1644, Parliament issued the charter in favor of "Providence Plantations." This was the colony which later was to be called Rhode Island.

One day at the close of the following autumn, the waters around Providence were crowded with canoes. Many of the people in the colony had left their work in the fields. They were out to meet Roger Williams on his return from England. Their cheers shook the leaves of the forest and startled the deer and wild turkeys.

Naturally the first question was about the charter.

"Here it is," said Mr. Williams, holding the document aloft.

This time the shouting must have reached even the clams in their beds of sand.

Mr. Williams told the story of his tour.

Yes, he seemed to have succeeded in his mission. The trouble was that the new English government was shaky. No one knew how far the people would go in their revolution. For instance, waiting for a boat, Roger Williams had written a

pamphlet, or small book. In it he stated that all government depended on the consent of the people. He said that it was the duty of government to protect every person's right to his own beliefs. He thought that the English people would applaud his pamphlet.

Maybe the people would have, but Parliament ordered it burned. Roger feared that the leaders then in charge of the English government could not be depended on. They might not stand back of the charter for Providence Plantations, but for the time being, the colony was safe.

Not for long. It happened that a group of people of the Baptist religion came to Boston. In Boston it was considered a crime to differ from the Massachusetts church, and the Baptists were called criminals. The magistrates ordered them whipped, fined, put in jail, or thrown out of Massachusetts. A number of them fled to Providence Plantations, where they were welcome. The general court of Massachusetts declared that the charter which Roger Williams had obtained did not give his colony the right to receive "enemies of God." In the name of the Lord they demanded that the Baptists be punished or returned to Massachusetts for punishment. Roger Williams, who had been elected governor of the new colony, refused.

"When people use the name of the Lord to justify hurting others," he said shrewdly, "it is because they want something for themselves."

He was right. The Bay Colony soon laid claim to some land near Providence and threatened to send soldiers to take it by force. To make matters worse, the court kept stirring up one tribe of Indians against another. Indian wars would give them the excuse to send troops into the fertile lands they wanted. Once they threatened to attack Roger Williams's neighbors, Sachem Canonicus and his tribe.

"What will you gain by war?" urged Roger Williams. "Plague, destruction, death. All of us have had to leave England. Remember that the Indians have been kinder to us than our own people have been."

Several times he succeeded in preventing war, but the citizens of his colony were worried. They saw the danger to their shelter for the poor and persecuted. They would be safe only when the English government gave them another charter. This time the charter must make it clear what the rights of the colony were. It must be as clear as a huge sign which might have read: "This colony is a democracy."

In June, 1651, Roger Williams and a friend sailed for England, where they found that the civil war was going very well for the people. The general of the forces of Parliament was Oliver Cromwell, whom Roger had known as a young man. Roger found much more freedom in England than ever before. Many religious sects were openly practicing their faith. Roger had high hopes for success when he laid his claim for a new charter before a commission of Parliament.

Then suddenly, everything changed. All of his hopes were dashed. Cromwell seized the entire government. He dismissed Parliament in 1653 and became dictator. The decision on the charter rested in his hands.

Then Roger Williams knew the liberties of his colony were still not safe. Who could tell what a dictator would or would not do? After three anxious years in England, he boarded a ship for home.

"The Charter Has Come!"

The Williams family was eight strong. By the time the father returned in 1653, Mary was a young lady of twenty. Freeborn was eighteen. The younger children—Providence, Mercy, Daniel, and Joseph—ranged all the way from fifteen years down to nine. It was lucky that their mother had six children to help her run the farm. Crops had to be sown and harvested. Herds of cattle had to be cared for.

Even after Roger Williams returned to America, he was away from home more than he was there. The children could not understand why he must be gone so much. For several years he served as president of the colony, and there was always something or other to take him away from his family.

For instance, there was the Verin case. Mr. Verin had come from Massachusetts so that he might have freedom to practice his own religion. Fine! There were a number of different churches in the colony. But when Mrs. Verin, his wife, wanted to go to a church different from her husband's, Mr. Verin put his foot down. A woman had no right to differ with her husband, he insisted.

Well, President Williams had to explain patiently that in Providence a woman had the same rights as a man. He had to explain that democracy wasn't beautiful only because one had many rights. Mr. Verin had duties, too. One of his duties was to protect other people's rights, including his wife's, even if he did not agree with her.

Mr. Williams sometimes had to go tramping through the woods for days or sailing out into the bay to talk with some Indian sachem. Slowly, surely, the poor Indian was being squeezed out by the white man, and his lands taken from him. Mr. Williams did all in his power to protect his Indian neighbors. When the Indian became desperate about losing his land and started on the warpath, Roger Williams would suddenly appear. The Indian might be angry with the whole white race, but he could not be angry with Mr. Williams.

"Let us try the civilized way of peaceful talk and compromise," said Mr. Williams every time.

He was a regular visitor in the Indian villages. He smoked with the sachems and gave them advice in their dealings with the English colonies. If a child had a fever, Mr. Williams came to bring him medicine. If a warrior had trouble with a wound, Mr. Williams brought bandages and dressed the wound.

The Williams children did not see their father as often as they wished even when he was in Providence. He spent much of his time writing or meeting with other officials in the colony. Everybody was worried about the charter. What if the English government denied the colony a new charter? What if Massachusetts and the other New England colonies were given the right to take over Providence Plantations? What would happen to the people who had sought safety there?

Where, for instance, would Mr. Solomon Franco find refuge? He had come from Holland, hoping to make his home in Boston. Perhaps he expected that the people in the Bay Colony would remember how kind the Dutch people had been to the Pilgrims. Not when they found that Mr. Franco's religion was Jewish! The magistrates of Boston studied Hebrew and read their Bible over and over. Part of the Bible had been written by the Jews. Yet the magistrates arrested Mr. Franco and drove him from the colony.

Jews had been driven from most of the countries in Europe.

They also had been driven from Brazil.

They had been driven from Peru.

They had been driven from Mexico.

But when they came to Roger Williams's colony, they found that their faith was respected. A synagogue, or Jewish church, was founded in Newport in 1658.

"More outcasts in Providence Plantations," sneered the magistrates of the Bay Colony. They became more determined to destroy the settlement.

In July, 1656, two women landed in Boston. They belonged to a religious group called Friends, or Quakers. When they tried to preach, they were seized by officers and driven from the colony. More Quakers landed. They were whipped and sent to jail. People who even spoke in a friendly way to Quakers were punished. Some Quakers were hanged. Up and down the coast of the New World, the Quakers had been driven out.

They had been driven from Virginia.

They had been driven from Maryland.

They had been driven from New Netherland.

They had been driven from Massachusetts.

They had heard of Roger Williams's colony. It happened that he himself did not like the Quakers and their ways, but

North

West · East

South

Salem—

Boston

Plymouth—

Providence

Warwick

Newport
Portsmouth

NEW
ENGLAND
Settlements
17th Century

he insisted that everyone had a right to his own religion. When the Quakers arrived as refugees, they found respect for their faith.

In a fury the magistrates of Massachusetts demanded that Providence Plantations stop receiving "this riffraff," as they called the Quakers.

"We have no law to punish people for declaring their minds concerning the ways of God," replied the president of the colony.

Roger Williams continued to worry about the charter, especially after Oliver Cromwell died in 1658. The new Parliament invited Charles Stuart, the son of Charles I, to become king of England. For four anxious years Providence and the neighboring settlements waited for a decision from King Charles II.

The great news finally came on November 24, 1663. A new charter had been brought from England. Across fields hurried the people. They gathered in the meeting house in Newport. Some had scars across their necks, where they had been whipped before joining the colony. Others had the letter H (heretic) branded into the flesh of their hands. Still others had no right ears.

The president of the colony held up the king's charter as high as he could reach, so that every toddling child might see it. It united the settlements under the name, "Rhode Island and Providence Plantations." Later the name of the colony was to be shortened to Rhode Island.

Then the president read every word of the charter to the spellbound people. The charter was like a sign which said: "This colony shall be a democracy, where every man shall have a right to his own conscience."

35

While the words rang out, everyone turned to look at a white-haired man who had been saying such things ever since he was a youth in London. Nowhere in the world had a Rhode Island been believed possible. "Now even a king approves it," the people thought.

Until the end of Roger Williams's life in 1683, he was the champion of liberty. After he died his influence lived on. In time Rhode Island and twelve other colonies declared their independence of England and became a nation—the United States of America.

The men who worked out the Constitution, or plan of government for the new nation, remembered the fight which he and others like him had made for liberty. An amendment was added to the Constitution which promised that every American citizen should have the right to worship God in the way that he thought right. Other amendments said that every American might speak as he wished, might write as he wished, so long as he did not hurt others.

The liberties which Americans enjoy today are due in part to Roger Williams.

The quotations set off by boldface quotation marks (") are the words used by historical characters. Sometimes a quotation has been shortened or slightly adapted to the vocabulary of young readers, but the meaning and style of the original have been carefully preserved.

In a few places the author has told what the character might have said under known circumstances in order to make the biography more vivid. Such imagined conversation is indicated by regular quotation marks (").

PICTURE CALENDAR OF ROGER WILLIAMS AND HIS TIMES

1603   ROGER WILLIAMS WAS BORN IN LONDON
William Shakespeare was writing his famous plays and poems.
Queen Elizabeth of England died.
Captain John Smith escaped from the Turks.
Four years later the London Company established a trading colony in Virginia (1607).

1620   ROGER WORKED FOR SIR EDWARD COKE ABOUT THIS TIME
The first legislature in America, called the House of Burgesses, had been formed in Virginia the year before (1619).
Also the year before, the first Negroes were brought to the American colonies (1619).
Settlers, later called Pilgrims, landed in Plymouth (Mass.)

1631   ROGER WILLIAMS LANDED IN THE NEW WORLD
The city of Boston had been founded the year before (1630).

1636   WILLIAMS FOUNDED THE SETTLEMENT OF PROVIDENCE
The colony of Maryland was two years old.
Harvard College was founded.
The next year Japan barred most foreigners from entering their country (1637).

1643   WILLIAMS SOUGHT HELP FROM THE KING
Sir Isaac Newton, who later discovered the law of gravity, was one year old.
Louis XIV, aged five years, became king of France.
The next year William Penn was born (1644).
Four years later Peter Stuyvesant began his rule as governor of New Netherland (1647).

**1653-
1682**   ROGER WILLIAMS WORKED FOR RELIGIOUS TOLERANCE
Miles Standish died in Massachusetts (1656).
Charles Perrault was writing *Cinderella, Puss in Boots, Little Red Riding Hood,* and other stories for children.
The Carolina colonies were started (1663).
Peter Stuyvesant surrendered New Netherland to the English (1664).
The great fire of London destroyed nearly the whole city (1666).
La Salle reached the Gulf of Mexico and named the land Louisiana after King Louis of France (1682).

1683   ROGER WILLIAMS DIED
Sir Christopher Wren, the famous English architect, was designing beautiful buildings.
William Penn signed a treaty with the Indians and bought some of their land.

REAL PEOPLE

1